In the early nineteenth century, dancers began to wear the very short, fluffy ballet skirt which you see in the picture. It is called the *classic tutu*. The longer ballet skirt, ending above the ankle, is called the *romantic tutu*.

Beginners in Ballet

This ballet student is in the dressing room getting ready for her class. Through the open door you can see the big dance studio, with its huge mirrors and practice bar along the wall. Several of the students are beginning to do *pliés* (knee bends) at the bar.

Every class begins with these exercises to warm up and stretch the muscles. Grown-up, professional ballet dancers warm up by doing the very same exercises. A dancer's muscles must be properly exercised before each class and before each performance in order to avoid strain.

The girl at the right is wearing a practice suit. This is called a *leotard*. These brief knit practice suits make it easy for the teacher to see each movement. Some pupils, like the girl on the opposite page, wear skirts over their *leotards*, but though the skirt looks pretty, it may hide serious mistakes.

The Five Positions

The girls and boys; standing before their teacher, show that they know the five positions of the feet. These positions are the very first things to learn. Here the young dancers show the positions in order, from the boy on the left (in *first position*) to the girl at the extreme right (in *fifth position*). All ballet steps, no matter how complicated, start from one of the five positions. You can see, therefore, that it is very important to learn them properly.

Teacher

Onlooker in
second position

First position

Second position

These young ballet students wear soft practice slippers. They will continue to dance in soft slippers for several years, until their muscles are strong enough to advance to blocked toe slippers. See how all feet are in the turned-out position, the legs turning outward from the hips. This basic dancing posture helps them to balance as they leap and whirl. It difficult for beginners, but soon begins to seem quite natural.

Third position

Fourth position

Fifth position

Fourth
position

Battement tendu

Battement tendu

Practice Makes Perfect

Many experts feel that the best time to begin ballet lessons is when you are eight or a bit older. Good training in ballet will make you graceful and teach you to stand tall and straight. But again, little dancers are warned not to wear blocked toe slippers and not to get up on their toes until their muscles are strong enough—usually not before the age of ten.

The girl on the opposite page who has her foot hooked over the bar is *stretching,* while the boy in front is practicing a *step of elevation* (a leap). Notice how the students give special attention to the *port de bras* (the way the arms are held); a graceful arm position is most important for beautiful dancing.

A dancer must remember so many things—the way the legs and feet move, the arm position, the carriage of the head, and even the expression of the face!

Stretching
on bar

Ballotté
(to toss or leap)

Fourth position

Battement jeté

Battement jeté

The Language of Ballet

When you see ballet on the stage, in the movies, or on television, you will find it lots of fun to call the various steps and movements by their names.

Most special ballet words are French, the language of ballet. As the art first grew up in France, it was taught around the world by French dancing masters, who naturally used their own language in naming the steps.

The children above are practicing *ronds de jambe à terre*, a step in which the foot draws an invisible "D" shape on the floor. When they have repeated this movement with one foot for a while, they will practice with the other foot. All steps are practiced alternately with the right and left foot.

The two girls are practicing the *frappé* to the side, a quick strike or beat. The boy is doing a *grand battement*, a big kick. Both steps are done to the front, side, and back. The girl below does an exercise to stretch her muscles.

Frappé

Frappé

Grand battement

The pianist helps the ballet class greatly in learning to do all movements smoothly and rhythmically. Later on, when the students perform actual ballets, they will work even more closely with music.

Stretching leg muscles

Enjoying Ballet

The person who works out the dances is called the *choreographer*, and the person who writes the music is known as the *composer*. The composer and choreographer often work closely together, trying to match the spirit of music and the dance.

The girls at the right front are spinning across the floor *sur le pointes* (on the tips of the toes). The step they are using is called a *fouetté*. The boy at the top is supporting his partner's *arabesque* (one type of ballet pose).

When a ballerina whirls across the floor, you may wonder why she doesn't slip. Two reasons are shown at the top left: (1) she darns the toes of her slippers for a better grip; (2) she steps in the rosin box to coat the soles with non-skid rosin.

Fouetté

Supported
Arabesque

Fouetté

Fouetté

She has another trick, too, called spotting. She keeps her bearings by looking at a certain spot each time she turns. That's why a dancer's face seems to look out at the audience, as she turns, snapping quickly around again and again.

The Seven Movements

There are seven basic movements in dancing. These are as follows: to slide, to jump, to dart, to raise, to bend, to stretch, and to turn round. Here are examples of these movements, together with their French names.

How to pronounce some of the French words used in this book:

arabesque – ar-a-besk
ballotté – bal-o-tay
Fouetté – foo-ay-tay
Frappé – fra-pay
plié – plee-ay
relevé – rel-vay
jeté – zhe-tay
leotard – lee-o-tard

pas de deux – pa de du
pas de quatre – pa de katr
battement jeté – bat-mah zhe-tay

battement tendu – bat-mah tahn-du
grand battement – grahn bat-mah

glisser – glee-sir
sauter – so-ter
élancer – ay-Iahn-sir
relever – rel-ver
plier – plee-er
entendre – ay-tahn-dre
tourner – toor-ner

Slide
Glisser

Jump
Sauter

Dart
Élancer

Raise
Relever

Bend
Plier

Stretch
Étendre

Turn round
Tourner

Carriage of the Arms
Port de Bras

These are grouped in a famous movement of the *Pas de Quatre*. This is a good example of how the arms should be used: as a graceful, natural looking part of each step.

Pleasing movement of the arms is essential to good dancing. Elbows should be rounded softly, the hands should always look relaxed and natural, following the direction of the arms. It is wrong to crook the fingers or wrists, or try too hard to be graceful; too much effort will "break the line" of the position and produce an effect of strain.

Steps of Elevation

This ballet tells the fairy tale of Cinderella. On these two pages Cinderella dances two steps of *elevation* (leaps), first in her rags, then in riches with her Prince.

Many ballets have been made from fairy tales. The dances for such ballets are often based on folk dances and the music sometimes uses folk tunes. The costumes resemble the clothes of the country and time in which the story is supposed to take place. And the settings are, of course, painted with scenes which carry out the same idea.

One *choreographer* said that a ballet is like a colorful painting that has come to life, showing us how real people act and feel at a certain time and place. In this sense, the ballet is very much like a stage play or a movie, except that the story is told with lovely dancing and music.

These pictures show
THE FIVE POSITIONS
of the feet. Every
BALLET STEP
starts from one
of these positions.

COPYRIGHT © 2014, BLUE LANTERN STUDIO

ISBN/EAN: 9781595838353

FIRST PRINTING · PRINTED IN CHINA THROUGH COLORCRAFT LTD., HONG KONG · ALL RIGHTS RESERVED

THIS PRODUCT CONFORMS TO CPSIA 2008